QUICK AND EASY
MAIN MEALS

Spend less time in the kitchen with these fast and fuss-free main meals. From winter warmers to light supper suggestions and treats for special occasions, there's something delicious here for everyone to look forward to at the end of another busy day.

To make life easier it is a good idea to keep a store of canned and frozen foods on hand – they are always good in an emergency, eggs and cheese are also good standbys. Timesavers that every busy cook should make use of are things such as buying meat, chicken and fish prepared for cooking. A food processor is the ultimate timesaver in the kitchen, ingredients can be grated, shredded, chopped, blended, mixed and puréed in a fraction of the time it takes to do it by hand. Cooked rice and pasta freeze well and can be quickly reheated in the microwave, so cook extra to have on hand to use in dishes that require cooked rice or pasta or as an extra quick accompaniment to a meal. Encouraging other members of the family to help with meal preparation will also ease the pressure on you.

Try these simple, tasty dishes for speedy meals that are guaranteed to leave you with time to spare and are sure to please.

CONTENTS

FAMILY CHOICE

Tried and trusted family favourites such as Beef Stroganoff and Crisp Fried Chicken are featured here, as well as exciting new combinations like Lamb Chops en Croûte, Beef Patties with Horseradish Sauce and Apricot Chicken Coriander.

Apricot Chicken Coriander

A springtime salad which is simply delicious. The breast of the chicken is poached in the juice of canned apricots.

440g (14oz) canned apricot halves, drained, juice reserved

125ml (4fl oz) lemon or orange juice

375ml (12fl oz) water

1 tspn ground coriander

4 boneless chicken breast fillets

125g (4oz) mangetout

1 medium red pepper

Coriander Dressing

60ml (2fl oz) lemon or orange juice

60ml (2fl oz) olive oil

2 tblspn chopped fresh or 2 tspn ground coriander

freshly ground black pepper

1 Combine apricot juice, lemon or orange juice, water and coriander in a saucepan and bring to the boil. Add chicken fillets, lower heat and simmer for 10 minutes. Cover pan, remove from heat and set aside for 1 hour.

2 Cut mangetout and red pepper into strips. Plunge into boiling water for 2 minutes, drain and rinse in cold water. Arrange in a serving bowl with apricot halves.

3 Cut chicken across the grain into thin strips and toss carefully through salad.

4 To make dressing, place lemon or orange juice, oil, coriander and black pepper to taste in a bowl and whisk to combine. Drizzle dressing over salad and serve with thin cucumber sandwiches.

Serves 6

Variation
Substitute 440g (14oz) canned peach slices for the apricots.

Italian Haricot Salad

630g (20oz) canned beans selected from red kidney, borlotti, butter or cannellini, drained

2 firm-ripe tomatoes, peeled and quartered

2-3 dill pickles or Italian pickles, sliced

12 olives, black or green, halved

4 anchovy fillets

6 sun-dried tomatoes, halved, optional

1 tblspn capers

salt

freshly ground black pepper

125ml (4fl oz) mayonnaise

220g (7oz) can tuna in olive oil, chilled

fresh parsley or mixed herbs

1 Place beans, tomatoes, pickles, olives, anchovies, sun-dried tomatoes (if using) and capers in a bowl and toss to combine. Season with salt and black pepper and chill.

2 Just before serving, mix mayonnaise through salad and top with tuna in olive oil, lightly flaked and parsley or herbs.

Serves 4-6

Italian Haricot Salad, Beans in Tuna, Salmon Puffs, Apricot Chicken Coriander, Sweetcorn Soup

Beans in Tuna

A perfect light lunch dish made from ingredients on the pantry shelf. You may vary the canned beans used. A three-bean mix is one idea.

375g (12oz) canned cannellini beans, drained

375g (12oz) canned red kidney beans, drained

125ml (4fl oz) olive oil

juice of 1 lemon

2 cloves garlic, crushed

salt

freshly ground black pepper

1 red onion, thinly sliced or 6 spring onions, chopped

220g (7oz) canned tuna, drained and flaked

chopped fresh parsley or alfalfa sprouts

4 small pitta bread rounds

60g (2oz) butter, melted

1 Place beans in a bowl and mix with combined olive oil, lemon juice, garlic, salt and black pepper. Stir in red onion or spring onions and tuna. Sprinkle with parsley or alfalfa sprouts.

2 To serve, brush pitta bread rounds with melted butter and toast for 1-2 minutes each side. Cut in half, open to make pockets and fill with tuna mixture.

Serves 4

Salmon Puffs

220g (7oz) canned pink or red salmon, drained and flaked

90g (3oz) fresh breadcrumbs

6 spring onions, chopped

1 tblspn lemon juice

2 tblspn melted butter

salt

freshly ground black pepper

2 eggs, beaten

375ml (12fl oz) hot milk

1 Preheat oven to 180°C (350°F/ Gas 4). Place salmon, breadcrumbs, spring onions, lemon juice, butter with salt and

black pepper to taste in a bowl. Combine eggs and hot milk and beat into salmon mixture.

2 Spoon mixture into four buttered 250ml (8fl oz) ramekins or soufflé dishes. Alternatively, bake in a 1 litre (1³/₄pt) baking dish.

3 Arrange dishes in a shallow pan of water and bake for 30 minutes or until puffy and just set. Serve in dishes set on warmed entrée or dinner plates.

Serves 4

Sweetcorn Soup

30g (1oz) butter

1 onion, chopped

2 potatoes, diced

2 tblspn plain flour

500ml (16fl oz) milk

500ml (16fl oz) water

1 bay leaf

salt

ground white pepper

630g (20oz) canned sweetcorn, drained

2 tblspn cream

2 rashers bacon, fried and crumbled, to garnish

1 Melt butter in a saucepan, add onion and cook for 5 minutes, without browning. Add potatoes and cook for 2 minutes longer.

2 Stir flour into the mixture, then gradually add the milk and water, stirring constantly. Bring to the boil and add the bay leaf and salt and white pepper to taste. Add half the sweetcorn, cover and simmer for 15-20 minutes. Remove the bay leaf and discard. Remove pan from heat and set aside to cool slightly.

3 Transfer sweetcorn mixture to a blender or food processor and process until smooth. Return to a clean pan, add remaining sweetcorn and heat through. Stir in the cream, sprinkle with bacon and serve immediately.

Serves 4-6

Creamed Asparagus and Eggs Au Gratin

A dish that can be prepared ahead and refrigerated until required. Makes a tasty light meal when served with a green or mixed salad and hot French bread.

45g (1¹/₂oz) butter

3 tblspn plain flour

2 x 440g (14oz) canned asparagus spears or cuts, drained, liquid reserved

250ml (8fl oz) milk

salt

freshly ground black pepper

pinch cayenne pepper

6 hard-boiled eggs, quartered

90g (3oz) dry breadcrumbs

2 tspn butter, extra

1 Preheat oven to 180°C (350°F/Gas 4). Melt butter in a saucepan, add flour, blend well and cook for 1 minute over a gentle heat. Combine asparagus liquid and enough milk to measure 500ml (16fl oz), add to pan, stirring constantly. Bring slowly to simmering and cook until thickened.

2 Season mixture with salt, black pepper and cayenne pepper. Lightly butter a 1-1.25 litre (1³/₄-2pt) ceramic baking dish, pour in a thin layer of sauce (about one-third), then top with half the asparagus and half the eggs. Repeat layers and finish with a layer of sauce.

3 Sprinkle with breadcrumbs and dot with butter. Bake for 20 minutes, allowing an extra 10 minutes if the dish has been refrigerated before baking.

Serves 4-6

Chicken with Sweet Peppers

Chicken with Sweet Peppers

6 tblspn olive oil

6 chicken pieces

1 onion, cut into eighths

3 cloves garlic, crushed

1 red pepper, seeded and sliced into strips

1 yellow or green pepper, seeded and sliced into strips

750g (1½lb) tomatoes, peeled and chopped

1 tblspn sweet ground paprika

125ml (4fl oz) dry white wine

200g (6½oz) natural yogurt

chopped fresh parsley, for garnish

1 Heat half the oil in a saucepan over a medium heat, add the chicken pieces and cook until golden brown on both sides. Remove and set aside to keep warm.

2 Add onion, garlic, red and yellow or green peppers to pan and sauté for 5 minutes or until soft. Add tomatoes, paprika and wine and mix well. Return the chicken pieces to the pan, spoon sauce over and simmer, covered for about 30 minutes or until the chicken is tender.

3 To serve, arrange chicken in a warm serving dish or on warmed serving plates, drizzle with yogurt in a decorative fashion and scatter with chopped parsley.

Serves 4-6

Zippy Macaroni Cheese

315g (10oz) macaroni (elbows, small shells, tubes etc.)

440g (14oz) canned condensed cream of asparagus or celery soup

½ soup can milk

125g (4oz) grated Cheddar cheese

freshly ground black pepper

1 Cook macaroni according to packet directions and drain. Place soup and milk in a saucepan over a medium heat and stir until mixture comes to simmering.

2 Add cheese to pan and continue stirring until cheese has melted. Season to taste with black pepper, add macaroni and heat through. Serve sprinkled with a little paprika or chopped spring onion.

Serves 4-6

Sausage Pilau

500g (1lb) sausages

60g (2oz) butter

2 tspn curry powder

4 spring onions, finely chopped

330g (10½oz) long-grain rice, cooked

2 hard-boiled eggs, quartered

4 tblspn finely chopped fresh parsley

125ml (4fl oz) cream or evaporated milk

salt

freshly ground black pepper

lemon wedges, for garnish

1 Grill the sausages on both sides until golden brown and cooked through; cut into chunks and set aside.

2 Melt butter in a large, heavy frying pan and add the curry powder and spring onions. Stir over a low heat for 1 minute, then add rice, sausages, eggs, half the parsley and the cream. Continue stirring for 2-3 minutes or until heated through. Season to taste with salt and black pepper.

3 Spoon on to a heated serving dish, sprinkle remaining parsley over the top, and garnish with lemon wedges.

Serves 4-6

Pork Ball and Broccoli Soup

This soup makes a good start to an Oriental-style meal, a light luncheon or supper dish.

2 litres (3 1/2 pt) light chicken stock

2 leeks or 8 spring onions, thinly sliced

1 tspn finely chopped fresh ginger

2 tblspn rice wine or dry sherry

1 head broccoli, stems thinly sliced, heads broken into florets

1 carrot, thinly sliced

salt

freshly ground black pepper

Meatballs

375g (12oz) lean pork mince

4 spring onions, finely chopped

1 tspn finely chopped fresh ginger

1/2 tspn salt

1 tblspn cornflour

1 tblspn light soy sauce

1 egg, beaten

1 Place stock in a large saucepan, bring to the boil. Add leeks or spring onions, ginger, rice wine or dry sherry, broccoli, carrot with salt and black pepper to taste and bring back to the boil. Lower heat and simmer for 5 minutes.

2 To make meatballs, place pork, spring onions, fresh ginger, salt, cornflour, light soy sauce and egg in a bowl and mix together until well combined.

3 Form into small, marble-sized balls and drop into simmering soup. Cook for 3-4 minutes longer or until meatballs are cooked through.

Serves 6

Smoked Fish Chowder

500g (1lb) smoked cod or haddock

500ml (16fl oz) water

2 potatoes, diced

2 carrots, sliced

90g (3oz) frozen green peas

2 rashers bacon, diced

1 onion, chopped

500ml (16fl oz) milk or 375ml (12fl oz) milk and 125ml (4fl oz) double cream

1 Poach fish in simmering water for 5 minutes. Reserve liquid in pan, lift out fish, flake and set aside, discarding any bones and skin. Add potatoes, carrots and peas to reserved liquid in pan and simmer, covered, until tender.

2 Fry the bacon and onion in a separate pan until golden. Add to vegetables with fish and stir to combine. Heat the milk or milk and cream in a separate pan, add to the soup and reheat gently without boiling.

Serves 4-6

Chilli Beans and Beef

125g (4oz) macaroni, cooked until just tender

440g (14oz) canned spaghetti sauce with beef

315g (10oz) canned red kidney beans, drained

60ml (2fl oz) red wine

60g (2oz) grated Cheddar cheese

30g (1oz) butter

1/4 tspn chilli powder or Tabasco sauce (or to taste)

2 tblspn grated Cheddar cheese, extra

Place all ingredients, except extra cheese, in a saucepan and mix to combine. Heat gently, stirring occasionally, until mixture comes to simmering. Serve sprinkled with extra cheese.

Serves 4

Armenian Stuffed Cabbage

These cabbage leaf parcels are filled with a spicy Middle Eastern pilaf and simmered in chicken stock – a delicious winter warmer.

10-12 whole cabbage leaves

250ml (8fl oz) chicken stock

Herb and Nut Stuffing

125ml (4fl oz) olive oil

3 large onions, chopped

100g (3 1/2oz) rice

4 tblspn finely chopped fresh parsley

3 tblspn pistachio or pinenuts

3 tblspn tomato purée

125ml (4fl oz) water

1/4 tspn ground allspice

1/4 tspn ground cinnamon

1 tspn salt

1/4 tspn freshly ground black pepper

1 To make stuffing, heat the oil in a large frying pan, add onions and cook until soft and golden. Add rice, cover and cook on a low heat for about 5 minutes, stirring occasionally. Add remaining ingredients and cook for 5 minutes longer. Set aside to cool slightly.

2 To prepare the leaves for stuffing, drop them, 3 or 4 at a time, into a large saucepan of boiling water and cook for 2-3 minutes – just long enough to soften the leaves and make them pliable. Drain and flatten leaves and cut away thick centre vein.

3 Place a heaped tablespoon of filling on each leaf, tuck sides in, roll up lightly and lay, side-by-side, in a casserole dish which will hold them firmly packed so they stay in good shape.

4 Pour chicken stock over rolls, cover and simmer for 30 minutes or until filling is tender. Check occasionally and add a little water or extra stock, if drying out.

Serves 5-6

Crisp Fried Chicken

Serve with creamy mashed potatoes, a green salad and cooked corn on the cob.

6-8 chicken pieces

salt

freshly ground black pepper

plain flour, to coat

2 eggs, beaten

60g (2oz) breadcrumbs, made from stale bread

60g (2oz) grated Parmesan cheese

1/2 tspn ground ginger

3 tblspn vegetable oil

2 tblspn butter

lemon wedges or slices, for garnish

1 Preheat oven to 200°C (400°F/ Gas 6). Rub chicken pieces with salt and black pepper to taste and dust lightly with flour. Dip in eggs, then in combined bread-crumbs, cheese and ginger. Set aside in refrigerator to chill.

2 Heat oil and butter in a heavy frying pan and brown chicken pieces on all sides. Transfer chicken to roasting dish, and complete baking in oven for 20-25 minutes or until cooked through.

3 Serve with lemon wedges or overlap lemon slices on edge of serving dish. Lemon juice should be squeezed over chicken at table.

Serves 6

Salmon Potato Cakes

500g (1lb) cold mashed potato

220g (7oz) canned salmon, drained and flaked

1 egg, beaten

2 tblspn chopped fresh parsley

2 tblspn snipped fresh chives

1 tspn celery seeds

salt

freshly ground black pepper

1 tblspn butter

2 tspn vegetable oil

Crisp Fried Chicken

1 Place potato, salmon, egg, parsley, chives, celery seeds with salt and black pepper to taste in a bowl and mix to combine. Form mixture into four flat cakes about 7.5cm (3in) in diameter.

2 Heat butter and oil together in frying pan over a medium heat and cook cakes for 3 minutes each side or until golden and heated through.

Serves 4

Continental Sausages

2 tblspn olive oil

125g (4oz) bacon, diced

250g (8oz) onions, sliced

750g (1 1/2lb) old potatoes, cubed

1 tspn ground paprika

1/4 tspn caraway seeds, optional

375ml (12fl oz) beef stock or water

1 tblspn vinegar

salt

freshly ground black pepper

15g (1/2oz) butter

1/2 cabbage, shredded

4-6 Continental frankfurters or kransky sausages

1 Heat oil in a large saucepan over a medium heat, add bacon and cook for 2-3 minutes. Add onions and continue cooking, stirring, until golden brown. Add potatoes, paprika, caraway seeds (if using), stock or water, vinegar with salt and black pepper to taste. Bring to the boil, reduce heat and simmer, covered, for 30 minutes.

2 To make buttered cabbage, melt butter in a large separate pan, add cabbage, cover and cook gently for 10 minutes, tossing every 3 minutes. Remove and set aside to keep warm.

3 Cut frankfurts diagonally into chunks, add to onion and potato mixture and simmer 3 minutes longer or until heated through. Serve with buttered cabbage.

Serves 4-6

Stir Fry Beef and Peppers

Stir frying is a marvellous and quick way to produce a delicious meal in next to no time – something we have learned from the Chinese. Serve with steamed rice or boiled noodles.

250g (8oz) rump or round steak, trimmed and thinly sliced

1/2 tspn salt

2 tspn sugar

1 tblspn cornflour

1 tblspn rice wine or sherry

1/2 tspn chilli sauce, optional

freshly ground black pepper

3 tblspn vegetable oil

1 red or green pepper, sliced

1 tomato, cut into 6, or 8 cherry tomatoes, halved

4 spring onions, chopped

2 teaspoons finely chopped fresh ginger

1 tblspn soy sauce

1 Place steak in a bowl with salt, sugar, cornflour, wine or sherry, chilli sauce (if using) and black pepper. Toss well to combine and set aside to marinate for 20 minutes.

2 Heat 1 tablespoon oil in a wok or frying pan, add red or green pepper and tomato and stir fry for a few seconds over high heat. Remove from pan with a slotted spoon and set aside.

3 Heat remaining oil in the pan, add spring onions and ginger, then meat and stir fry for a few seconds before adding soy sauce. Return pepper and tomato mixture to pan, toss to combine and serve immediately.

Serves 4

Beef Stroganoff

2 fillet steaks, thinly sliced

2 tspn plain flour

salt

freshly ground black pepper

30g (1oz) butter

1 onion, chopped

6-8 button mushrooms, sliced, optional

1 tspn ground paprika

1 tspn tomato purée

125g (4oz) sour cream

1 Dust steak with flour and season with salt and black pepper.

2 Melt butter in a frying pan over a medium heat, add beef strips and onion and cook, tossing frequently, for 3 minutes or until golden brown. Add mushrooms (if using) and cook for 1 minute longer. Add paprika, tomato purée, and sour cream, toss to combine and heat through gently.

3 Serve with creamy mashed potato, toast points, potato straws, boiled rice or noodles. To keep warm, place stroganoff in a serving bowl and stand bowl in a pan of hot water for 10-15 minutes.

Serves 2

Lamb Chops en Croûte

A recipe from Provence, France. Thick lamb chops are grilled or barbecued and served on croûtes of fried or toasted French bread to catch the delicious juices.

4 thick lamb loin or chump chops

4 thick slices of bread

olive oil

1 onion, finely chopped

1 clove garlic, crushed

2 tblspn chopped fresh parsley

3 tblspn hot water

250ml (8fl oz) dry white wine

salt

freshly ground black pepper

extra chopped fresh parsley, for garnish

Lamb Chops en Croûte

Stir Fry Beef and Peppers

1 Grill chops under a preheated hot grill for about 4 minutes on each side, to produce meat that is well browned but pink in the centre. Grill for a few minutes longer if you want chops well done.

2 Meanwhile, lightly fry bread in a little olive oil in a frying pan until golden brown, drain on absorbent kitchen paper and set aside to keep warm.

3 Heat 2 tablespoons of olive oil in pan, add onion, garlic and parsley and fry until onion is golden brown. Add water and wine with salt and black pepper to taste and simmer for 5 minutes. To serve, place a lamb chop on top of each croûte, spoon over sauce and sprinkle with extra chopped parsley.

Serves 4

Beef Patties with Horseradish Sauce

Serve with creamy mashed potatoes or buttered noodles.

1kg (2lb) lean beef mince

salt

freshly ground black pepper

60g (2oz) breadcrumbs, made from stale bread

60g (2oz) butter, softened

3 tblspn snipped fresh chives

1 tblspn olive oil

chopped fresh parsley, for garnish

Horseradish Sauce

1 tblspn lemon juice

250ml (8fl oz) beef stock

125g (4oz) sour cream

2 tblspn grated fresh horseradish or 2 tspn bottled horseradish

1 Season meat with salt and black pepper and fork in breadcrumbs. Cream together butter and chives and combine with meat. The mixture should be handled lightly; do not compact it too much.

2 Shape mixture into six generous patties. Heat olive oil in a heavy frying pan, add patties and cook on a high heat for 5 minutes or until well browned, but still pink at the centre. Remove and set aside to keep warm.

3 To make sauce, place lemon juice and stock into the same frying pan and cook over a high heat until reduced to about half. Remove pan from heat and stir in sour cream. Return pan to a gentle heat and stir in horseradish to taste. Serve patties drizzled with sauce and sprinkled with chopped parsley.

Serves 6

WARM AND HEARTY

There's nothing nicer than the promise of a homecooked meal at the end of a busy day. Choose from Chilli Con Carne, Meatballs in Lemon Caper Sauce and Chicken with Bouillabaisse Sauce, amongst others. 'What's for dinner?' has never been simpler to answer.

Pork Steaks Stuffed with Mushrooms

30g (1oz) butter

1 onion, finely chopped

250g (8oz) mushrooms, finely chopped

salt

freshly ground black pepper

30g (1oz) breadcrumbs, made from stale bread

6 pork midloin butterfly steaks

60g (2oz) plain flour

45g (1½oz) butter

1 tblspn olive oil

250ml (8fl oz) dry white wine

3 tblspn sour cream

1 Melt butter in a pan over a medium heat, add onion and cook for 2-3 minutes. Add mushrooms, season to taste with salt and black pepper and cook until most of the moisture has evaporated. Stir in breadcrumbs and set aside to cool.

2 Divide mixture into six, spoon each portion in the centre of each butterfly steak and fold over to enclose. Use small poultry skewers or wooden toothpicks to secure.

3 Dust each steak with flour. Heat the butter and oil in a heavy nonstick frying pan, add the pork and cook until golden on each side. Add the wine and bring to the boil. Cover and simmer gently for 15-20 minutes, or until tender. Stir in sour cream. Serve pork drizzled with juices from pan.

Serves 6

Chilli-Bean Casserole

30g (1oz) butter

1 onion, finely chopped

750g (1½lb) lean beef mince

440g (14oz) canned tomatoes, drained and chopped

250ml (8fl oz) hot beef stock

125g (4oz) pasta shells, bows or macaroni tubes

1 tblspn chopped fresh mixed herbs or ½ tspn dried mixed herbs

1 tspn chilli powder

1 tspn Worcestershire sauce

salt and freshly ground black pepper

315g (10oz) canned red kidney beans, drained

finely chopped fresh parsley, for garnish

1 Melt butter in a saucepan over a medium heat, add onion, then mince and cook, stirring constantly to break up any large chunks, until well browned.

2 Stir in tomatoes, stock, pasta, herbs, chilli powder, Worcestershire sauce and salt and black pepper to taste and bring to simmering. Simmer gently for 30 minutes, adding more water and stirring as necessary.

3 When meat is cooked and pasta is tender, stir in kidney beans and heat through. To serve, sprinkle with chopped parsley.

Serves 6

Meatballs in Lemon Caper Sauce

375g (12oz) beef mince

375g (12oz) pork mince

3 slices stale white bread

250ml (8fl oz) lukewarm water

1 onion, finely chopped

3 anchovy fillets, chopped

2 eggs

1 tblspn chopped fresh parsley

1 tspn finely grated lemon rind

½ tspn salt

¼ tspn freshly ground black pepper

750ml-1 litre (1¼-1¾pt) beef stock

1 onion, whole

1 bay leaf

Lemon Caper Sauce

30g (1oz) butter

2 tspn finely chopped onion

1½ tblspn plain flour

2 tblspn lemon juice

2 tblspn capers

125g (4oz) sour cream

1 Place beef mince and pork mince in a bowl and mix to combine. Cut bread into small pieces and soak in lukewarm water for 15 minutes. Drain, squeeze dry and mix into meat mixture with chopped onion and anchovies. Add eggs, parsley, lemon rind with salt and black pepper to taste and mix well to combine. Shape mixture into 5cm (2in) balls.

2 Place stock, whole onion and bay leaf in a large saucepan and bring to simmering. Simmer for 10 minutes, drop in meatballs and simmer for 20 minutes or until meatballs rise to the surface. Using a slotted spoon, transfer meatballs to a heated dish, cover and set aside to keep warm. Reserve stock.

3 To make sauce, melt butter in saucepan, add onion and cook gently until translucent. Stir in flour and allow to brown very slowly. Pour in reserved stock and stir continuously until thickened. Add lemon juice and capers. Add meatballs and simmer very gently until heated through. Stir in sour cream and serve.

Serves 4-6

Pork Steaks Stuffed with Mushrooms

Chicken with Bouillabaisse Sauce

Chicken with Bouillabaisse Sauce

olive oil

2 onions, chopped

8 small chicken pieces such as drumsticks or thighs

salt

freshly ground black pepper

8 tomatoes, peeled, seeded and chopped

3 cloves garlic, finely chopped

small bouquet garni

1 strip orange rind

¹/4 tspn fennel seeds

15g (¹/2oz) butter

6 fresh basil leaves, chopped

¹/2 tspn saffron threads, optional

1 Heat 2 tblspn olive oil in a wide frying pan over a medium heat, add onions and cook until soft and golden; remove and set aside. Add chicken pieces to the same pan and cook until golden brown on all sides; season to taste with salt and black pepper.

2 Add the tomatoes, 2 of the chopped garlic cloves, bouquet garni, orange rind and fennel seeds and toss to combine. Cook, covered, for 15-20 minutes or until the chicken is tender.

3 Meanwhile, mash the butter with the remaining garlic, basil and saffron (if using). Using a slotted spoon, transfer the chicken pieces to a serving dish and set aside to keep warm. Whisk the flavoured butter into the sauce and gently heat through. To serve, pour sauce over the chicken.

Serves 4-6

Croque Monsieur

The French alternative to a hamburger. Just as good made at home as they are in Paris where they are sold in nearly every boulevard café. Use crusty French or Italian bread or a sandwich loaf.

8 slices of French bread

butter

a little French mustard

4 slices ham

4 slices Swiss-style cheese

freshly ground black pepper

1 Spread bread generously with butter, then spread four slices with a little mustard and top with ham, cheese, black pepper to taste and remaining bread slices.

2 Press sandwiches together firmly and trim the crust, if you like. Cut into two triangles, three fingers or halves lengthwise, or leave whole.

14

3 Melt a generous amount of butter in a frying pan over a medium heat. Add sandwiches and cook for 3-4 minutes on each side or until golden. Drain on absorbent kitchen paper and serve hot.

Serves 4

Variation

If you like, croques can be dipped into a mixture of 2 beaten eggs and 125ml (4fl oz) of milk, before frying as above.

Pasta Shells with Tomato Sauce

For the microwave. Cook the pasta in the regular way but make the most of your microwave by using it to make this tasty sauce.

2 litres (3¹/₂pt) water
1 tblspn olive oil
salt
250g (8oz) pasta bows
15g (¹/₂oz) butter
2 tblspn freshly grated Parmesan cheese

Tomato Sauce

1 onion, finely chopped
2 cloves garlic, crushed
440g (14oz) canned tomatoes, chopped, juice reserved and blended with 1 tspn cornflour
2 tspn chopped fresh oregano or ¹/₂ teaspoon dried oregano
2 tblspn tomato purée
freshly ground black pepper

1 Place the water in a large saucepan and bring to the boil. Stir in oil, salt and pasta and cook for 10-12 minutes or until *al dente*.

2 To make the sauce, place the onion and garlic in a microwavable bowl, cover and cook on HIGH (100%) for 2 minutes. Stir in the tomatoes and cornflour mixture, oregano, tomato purée with salt and black pepper to taste. Cook, uncovered, for 3 minutes longer, stirring after 1¹/₂ minutes.

3 Drain the pasta and stir in the sauce and butter. Sprinkle with Parmesan cheese and serve immediately.

Serves 4

Croque Monsieur

Mini Meat Loaves

These look wonderful popping out of a red pepper, although they can be made in muffin tins or any similar small containers. Any leftovers are good for the next day's lunch.

750g (1 1/2lb) beef mince

3 spring onions, finely chopped

1 clove garlic, crushed

1 egg

45g (1 1/2oz) dried breadcrumbs

2 tblspn fruit chutney

1 carrot, grated

1/2 tspn dried thyme

8 small or 4 medium red peppers

1 Preheat oven to 190°C (375°F/ Gas 5). Combine mince, spring onions, garlic, egg, breadcrumbs, fruit chutney, carrot and thyme in a bowl and mix well. Slice the tops off the peppers and scoop out the seeds or halve the medium peppers.

2 Divide the mince mixture into eight equal portions and form into cupcake shapes. Place each portion inside a pepper. Put the peppers in a greased baking dish and bake for 15-20 minutes or until cooked through.

3 Serve with 2 x 315g (10oz) cans of creamed corn heated in the microwave for 3 minutes and 4 jacket potatoes, cooked on HIGH (100%) in the microwave for 8 minutes, then baked for 10 minutes in a conventional oven, to crisp the skin. Serve 2 mini loaves per person.

Serves 4

Salmon Cakes with Tartare Sauce

Change these to crab cakes by using 440g (14oz) of canned crab meat and substituting fresh tarragon for the dill.

375g (12oz) potatoes

2 tblspn butter

440g (14oz) canned red salmon, drained

3 tblspn snipped fresh chives

2 tblspn chopped fresh parsley

2 tblspn chopped fresh dill

2 stalks celery, cut into 1cm (1/2in) lengths

3 tblspn mayonnaise

1 tblspn Dijon mustard

2 tspn Worcestershire sauce

1 egg

1/2 tspn Tabasco sauce

125g (4oz) dried breadcrumbs

2 extra eggs, beaten

2 tblspn light vegetable or olive oil

Tartare Sauce

250ml (8fl oz) mayonnaise

3 tblspn gherkin relish

2 tblspn capers, chopped

1 tblspn lemon juice

1 spring onion, sliced thinly

1 Cook potatoes in plenty of boiling water until soft; drain, transfer to a large mixing bowl and mash well with butter. Add salmon, chives, parsley, dill, celery, mayonnaise, mustard, Worcestershire sauce, egg, Tabasco sauce and 2 tblspn dried breadcrumbs and mix well to combine.

2 Shape mixture into eight patties, dip into beaten egg then coat with remaining breadcrumbs. Heat oil in a frying pan over a medium heat and cook patties until golden brown, turning once. Serve immediately with tartare sauce and a green salad.

3 To make sauce, place mayonnaise, relish, capers, lemon juice and spring onion in a bowl and mix well to combine.

Makes 8 patties

Vegetarian Pasta

A low-fat way to enjoy a pasta dish. Combine with any vegetables for a delicious meatless meal. The sauce can be used as a tasty substitute for full-fat cheese sauces in other dishes if you omit the basil and add 1 tablespoon of mild prepared mustard.

2 tblspn olive oil

1 onion, sliced

2 cloves garlic, chopped

1 red pepper, sliced

1/2 head cauliflower, cut in florets

1 head broccoli, cut in florets

220g (7oz) button mushrooms, sliced

2 tblspn chicken stock

500g (1lb) spaghetti

Cheesy Sauce

250g (8oz) cottage cheese

125ml (4fl oz) low fat milk

125g (4oz) sour cream

3 tblspn freshly grated Parmesan cheese

2 tblspn chopped fresh basil

1 Heat oil in wok over medium heat, add onion, garlic and red pepper and cook, stirring, for 3 minutes. Add cauliflower and broccoli and cook, stirring, for 5 minutes longer. Add mushrooms, toss to combine and pour in stock. Reduce heat, cover and cook for 5 minutes or until vegetables are tender.

2 Boil spaghetti in salted water until *al dente*. Drain and set aside to keep warm.

3 To make sauce, place cottage cheese, milk, sour cream, Parmesan cheese and basil in a food processor or blender and blend until smooth. Add sauce to pasta, mix to combine and toss through vegetables. Serve immediately.

Serves 4-6

Mini Meat Loaves

Sautéed Chicken with Potatoes and Peas

Sautéed Chicken with Potatoes and Peas

6 chicken pieces

3 tblspn olive oil

500g (1lb) potatoes, cut into chunks

2 cloves garlic, chopped

3 tomatoes, peeled and roughly chopped

125g (4oz) frozen green peas

salt

freshly ground black pepper

chopped fresh parsley, for garnish

1 Remove excess fat from chicken and wipe dry with absorbent kitchen paper. Heat oil in a large frying pan over a medium heat and fry the chicken pieces for 3-4 minutes on each side or until golden.

2 Add potatoes and garlic, toss to combine, cover tightly and cook for 10 minutes. Add tomatoes and cook for 10 minutes longer.

3 Add peas with salt and black pepper to taste, toss to combine. Cover and continue to cook until the chicken is tender and cooked through. Serve garnished with parsley.

Serves 6

Sausages with Apples

Good pork sausages are hard to beat for an easy meal. Serve with butter cooked apples, creamy mashed potatoes, or boiled rice.

8 pork sausages

1 tblspn vegetable oil

30g (1oz) butter

3 apples, cored and sliced

125ml (4fl oz) dry cider or white wine

1 tblspn brandy

125ml (4fl oz) cream

salt

freshly ground black pepper

1 Bring a large saucepan of water to the boil. Add sausages and simmer for 5 minutes. Drain sausages well and prick several times with a small sharp knife.

2 Heat oil in a frying pan over a medium heat and fry sausages until golden brown.

3 In another pan, melt butter and cook apples until golden. Remove apples and set aside to keep warm. Add cider or wine to pan, bring to the boil and boil until liquid reduces slightly. Reduce heat and stir in brandy and cream. Simmer sauce until thickened to desired consistency. Season to taste with salt and black pepper.

4 Serve sausages accompanied by apples and sauce.

Serves 4

Lamb Cutlets en Papillote

8 lamb cutlets, trimmed

freshly ground black pepper

185g (6oz) butter

1 tspn chopped fresh thyme or
¼ tspn dried thyme

4 tblspn shredded sorrel or basil or
chopped parsley

4 cloves garlic, crushed

salt

1 carrot, cut into julienne strips, blanched

1 leek, cut into julienne strips, blanched

4 large or 8 small button mushrooms, sliced

1 egg white

1 Preheat oven to 190°C (375°F/ Gas 5). Season cutlets with black pepper. Melt 60g (2oz) butter in frying pan over a medium heat, add cutlets and brown quickly on both sides. Remove and set aside.

2 Place 100g (3½oz) of the remaining butter in a bowl, add herbs and garlic and beat until smooth. Season to taste with salt and black pepper and set aside.

3 Melt the remaining butter in a frying pan, add blanched vegetables and mushrooms and stir fry for 1-2 minutes. Remove pan from heat and set aside.

4 From baking paper, cut out 4 large heart shapes, each about 25cm (10in) at its widest point. Spoon a quarter of the julienne vegetables on one half of each heart, leaving a good space around the edge. Lay two cutlets on top, then spoon over the mushrooms. Finish each with a spoon of the herbed butter.

5 To seal, brush the outside edge of each paper heart with egg white, fold over to encase the filling and press the edges together. Brush edge again with egg white and fold again. Repeat if necessary so that the parcel is completely sealed.

6 To cook, lay the parcels on a baking tray and bake for 20-30 minutes or until the parcels have puffed up and are nicely coloured. Arrange on plates and open at the table with a small sharp knife.

Serves 4

Chilli Con Carne

330g (10½oz) long-grain rice, washed

375ml (12fl oz) water

1 tspn salt

3 tblspn olive oil

750g (1½lb) lean beef mince

2 cloves garlic, chopped

salt

chilli powder

440g (14oz) canned peeled tomatoes and
their liquid

315g (10oz) canned red kidney beans,
drained

1 Place rice, water and salt into a saucepan, bring to the boil, stir once, lower heat, cover and simmer for 15 minutes or until rice is tender and liquid absorbed. Fluff up with a fork.

2 Meanwhile, heat oil in pan, add beef and garlic and stir fry for 5 minutes, breaking up mince with a fork to separate and adding salt and chilli powder, to taste (try 1-2 tspn milder Mexican chilli powder and ½-1 tspn other spicier varieties).

3 Stir in tomatoes and liquid, bring to the boil, lower heat and simmer for 10 minutes. Add kidney beans, stir to combine and cook for 15 minutes longer or until heated through. Serve with boiled rice.

Serves 4

Lamb Cutlets en Papillote

LIGHT AND EASY

Next time you're feeling peckish and can't think what to cook, take your pick from this selection of fast and fabulous ideas.

Grilled Skewered Pork Fillet

Ask an Italian delicatessen for prosciutto crudo (translates simply as ham raw) or pancetta, thinly sliced. Pork fillets are now readily available from supermarkets and butchers.

2 large or 3 small pork fillets

12 thin slices prosciutto or pancetta

8 thick slices Italian bread

4 tblspn olive oil

freshly ground black pepper

bruised fresh rosemary leaves

1 Wipe fillets with absorbent kitchen paper and cut into 24 thick slices. Halve the prosciutto or pancetta slices. Cut the bread slices into quarters or pieces just a little larger than the pork.

2 Thread the skewers first with a piece of bread, then a piece of the prosciutto folded over to approximately the same size, then a pork slice. Repeat sequence twice, ending with a fourth piece of bread. Repeat with remaining ingredients to make 8 skewers.

3 Brush skewers with a little oil and season to taste with black pepper and rosemary leaves. Cook over a preheated hot barbecue or under a grill for 8 minutes, turning frequently or until meat is cooked through and bread is crisp and golden. Serve immediately with a green salad.

Serves 4

Tomato and Bread Soup

This becomes a thick soup, made from fresh tomato and basil with plenty of garlic. Serve it at room temperature for a refreshing summer meal.

2 tblspn olive oil

2 cloves garlic, crushed

2 tblspn chopped spring onions

6-8 tomatoes, peeled, seeded and diced

8 fresh basil leaves, shredded

500ml (16fl oz) chicken stock

salt

freshly ground black pepper

4 slices rye or white bread, crusts removed, cut into cubes

shredded fresh basil and grated Parmesan cheese, for garnish

1 Heat the olive oil in a large pan. Add the garlic and spring onions and cook over a medium heat until softened, about 5 minutes. Add the tomatoes, basil and stock with salt and black pepper to taste. Stir and simmer gently for about 5 minutes.

2 Add the bread cubes to the soup and continue to simmer for 1 minute longer. Remove from the heat and cool at room temperature for about 30 minutes. Serve sprinkled with the extra shredded basil and grated Parmesan cheese.

Serves 4

Tomato and Bread Soup, Grilled Skewered Pork Fillet

Pastrami Rice Salad

8-10 slices pastrami or beef salami, cut into strips

220g (7oz) long-grain rice, cooked and cooled

250g (8oz) mixed, lightly steamed vegetables (choose from: broccoli florets, sugar snap peas, green peas, beans, carrot slices, red or green pepper)

2 tblspn pinenuts, toasted

6-8 black olives, halved and pitted

Mustard and Parsley Dressing

2 tblspn wine vinegar

1 tspn Dijon-style mustard

90ml (3fl oz) olive oil

2 tblspn chopped fresh parsley

freshly ground black pepper

1 To make dressing, place vinegar, mustard, oil, parsley and black pepper to taste in a screwtop jar and shake well to combine.

2 Combine half the pastrami or salami with the cooked rice, steamed vegetables and dressing. Cover and set aside at room temperature for 20-30 minutes.

3 Place rice salad into a salad bowl and top with remaining pastrami or salami strips, the pinenuts and black olives.

Serves 6-8

Danish Bacon and Egg Cake

When you have to draw on the refrigerator for a nourishing meal, make this omelette and serve with a salad and crusty bread.

4 rashers bacon

6 eggs

1¹/₂ tblspn plain flour

125ml (4fl oz) milk

salt

freshly ground black pepper

1 tblspn snipped fresh chives

1 Remove rind from bacon and cut each rasher into four. Fry bacon slowly in its own fat until crisp. Remove from pan, drain on absorbent kitchen paper and set aside to keep warm.

2 Place eggs in a bowl and beat lightly, beat in flour, add milk and season to taste with salt and black pepper.

3 Pour off all but 1 tablespoon fat from pan. Heat pan then pour in egg mixture. Cook for 1 minute, stirring gently, then cover pan and cook gently until eggs are just set.

4 Place bacon on top of omelette, sprinkle with chives and serve straight from the pan, cutting into 4 wedges.

Serves 4

Pastrami Rice Salad

Beef Salad with Cumin Vinaigrette

Beef Salad with Cumin Vinaigrette

6 slices corned silverside or lean roast beef

1 red or green pepper, cut into strips

1 courgette, sliced

¹/₂ onion or 6 spring onions, sliced

mixed salad greens, washed and crisped

3 tblspn chopped fresh coriander or mixed herbs

Cumin Vinaigrette

1 tblspn white wine vinegar

1¹/₄ tspn ground cumin

1 tspn Dijon-style mustard

60ml (2fl oz) olive oil

1 To make vinaigrette, place vinegar, cumin, mustard and oil in a screwtop jar and shake well to combine.

2 Cut meat into strips. Combine meat with red or green pepper, courgette and onion. Toss through vinaigrette. Cover and refrigerate until required.

3 Arrange salad greens on four dinner plates. Place beef salad on greens and sprinkle with coriander or herbs.

Serves 4

Cheesy Fish Puff

375g (12oz) prepared puff pastry

250g (8oz) cooked fish (cod, haddock, tuna or salmon)

60g (2oz) grated Cheddar cheese

2 large eggs, beaten

salt

freshly ground black pepper

pinch dried marjoram

1 Preheat oven to 220°C (425°F/ Gas 7). Roll pastry into an oblong about 30 x 20cm (12 x 8in), cut in half and place one half on a damp baking tray. Roll remaining pastry so that its size is increased by about 6mm (¹/₄in) on all sides.

2 Flake fish with a fork and place in a bowl. Add cheese and eggs, reserving about 1 tablespoon of egg for glazing later. Season to taste with salt, black pepper and marjoram. Spread mixture over the smaller piece of pastry, leaving a narrow border on all sides.

3 Cover with larger piece of pastry, pinching edges firmly together. Brush pastry with reserved beaten egg and set aside to stand in a cool place for at least 15 minutes. Bake for 20-25 minutes or until pastry is well risen and golden.

Serves 4

Chicken with Olives and Tomatoes

4 chicken breast halves

freshly ground black pepper

2 tblspn olive oil

15g (1/2oz) butter, melted

4 tomatoes, peeled, seeded and quartered

8 green olives

8 black olives

1 Preheat oven to 220°C (425°F/ Gas 7). Wipe chicken with absorbent kitchen paper and season well with black pepper. Place in a baking dish and drizzle with the oil. Bake, uncovered, for 15-20 minutes or until cooked through. Remove chicken and place on a heated serving dish, spoon over melted butter, set aside and keep warm.

2 Drain excess fat from baking dish and add tomatoes and olives. Return pan to the oven and bake for 5 minutes or until tomatoes are hot.

3 Arrange the tomatoes and olives around the chicken and drizzle over any juices remaining in the pan. Serve with steamed new potatoes or crusty bread.

Serves 4

Grilled Salmon Steaks

This is a luxury dish that is often found on top restaurant menus but one that you can master at home. Salmon may also be poached and served with the sauce.

4 x 155g (5oz) salmon cutlets or fillets, each about 2.5cm (1in) thick

1 tspn vegetable or olive oil

salt

freshly ground black pepper

1 quantity Buerre Blanc Tomate (recipe follows)

1 Preheat grill to hot. Brush the salmon on both sides with oil and sprinkle with salt and black pepper, to taste.

2 Place salmon under grill and cook for 4-5 minutes each side or until flesh flakes when tested with a fork. Serve with Buerre Blanc Tomate and steamed new potatoes.

Serves 4

Buerre Blanc Tomate

4 tblspn finely chopped spring onions

375ml (12fl oz) dry white wine

155g (5oz) butter, cut into large dice

salt

1 tomato, peeled, seeded and diced

6-8 green peppercorns

1 Combine the spring onions and wine in a saucepan and bring to the boil. Reduce heat and simmer until liquid has been reduced to 90ml (3fl oz). Continue cooking over low heat, stirring rapidly with a wire whisk, while adding butter, one piece at a time. Season to taste with salt and set aside.

2 Heat a little butter in a separate saucepan, add tomato and green peppercorns and heat through. Add tomato mixture to sauce, stir to combine and serve.

Fish Cutlets with Herb Lemon Butter

Any firm white fish can be used for this simple but delicious dish. Whether cooking in the microwave or the oven, take care not to overcook.

45g (11/2oz) butter

2 tblspn lemon·juice

4 fish cutlets (about 750g/11/2lb)

2 tblspn finely chopped fresh herbs

salt

freshly ground black pepper

1 Place butter and lemon juice in a shallow microwavable dish and cook on HIGH (100%) for 2 minutes. Place cutlets in dish with thin ends towards centre, cover and cook on HIGH (100%) for 5 minutes, turning once during cooking. Place fish on heated plates and keep warm.

2 Stir herbs, salt and black pepper to taste into juices remaining in dish, microwave for 20 seconds, spoon butter mixture over fish and serve immediately.

3 To cook in a conventional oven preheat to 180°C (350°F/Gas 4). Place cutlets in a baking dish, cover and bake for 25-30 minutes.

Serves 4

Ham and Pasta Salad

A colourful lunchtime salad with lots of appetite appeal. Change the look with the mood by using different-shaped pasta.

315g (10oz) pasta shells, spiral shapes or penne

1 head broccoli, cut into florets

2 thick slices cooked ham, cut into strips

8 black olives, halved and stoned

2 stalks celery, sliced

125ml (4fl oz) thick mayonnaise

2 tspn Dijon mustard

salt

freshly ground black pepper

2 tblspn snipped fresh chives, chopped basil or chopped parsley

2 canned red peppers, drained and sliced

1 Cook pasta in boiling, salted water for about 10 minutes or until *al dente.* Drain and refresh under cold running water.

2 Blanch broccoli in boiling water for 1-2 minutes or until just softened but still firm to the bite. Drain and refresh under cold running water.

3 Mix ham with olives, celery, pasta and broccoli. Combine mayonnaise and mustard and season to taste with salt and black pepper. Add just enough mayonnaise to the salad to bind ingredients together. Cover and chill for 30 minutes. Just prior to serving, scatter with chives, basil or parsley and garnish with red pepper strips.

Serves 4

Chicken Saltimbocca

Chicken Saltimbocca

Traditionally made with very thin veal steaks in Italy, where 'saltimbocca' means 'jump in the mouth', because it's so quick to prepare.

4 boneless chicken breast fillets

60g (2oz) piece fresh Parmesan cheese, cut into 8 thin slices

8 slices prosciutto

8 fresh sage leaves

60g (2oz) butter

freshly ground black pepper

125ml (4fl oz) dry white wine, optional

1 Using a sharp knife split each breast fillet horizontally in two to make 8 thin steaks. Place a thin slice of Parmesan cheese in the centre and top each with a slice of prosciutto. Place a sage leaf in the centre and carefully secure with a wooden toothpick or cocktail stick.

2 Melt butter in a large frying pan over a medium heat, add chicken pieces and brown quickly, a few minutes on each side or until cooked through. Season to taste with black pepper, arrange on a serving dish and set aside to keep warm.

3 Add wine (if using) to pan and scrape base well, adding a small nut of butter for a richer sauce. Drizzle sauce over chicken pieces and serve immediately.

Serves 4

Beef in Black Bean Sauce

Black beans are available from Oriental food stores and some supermarkets.

1 tblspn salted black beans

500g (1lb) lean rump steak

1/2 tspn salt

1/2 tspn bicarbonate of soda

60ml (2fl oz) water

1 egg white

1 tblspn cornflour

vegetable oil

1 onion, chopped

1 green pepper, sliced

2 cloves garlic, crushed

freshly ground black pepper

Soy and Sherry Sauce

1 tspn sugar

1 tspn cornflour

2 tspn soy sauce

1 tblspn dry sherry

60ml (2fl oz) water

1 Place black beans in cold water and set aside to soak for 1 hour or longer. Cut steak into strips 5cm (2in) long and 1cm (1/2in) wide and place in a bowl with salt, bicarbonate of soda, water, egg white and cornflour. Mix well to combine, cover and refrigerate for at least 1 hour.

Ham and Pasta Salad (page 24)

2 Heat 1 tblspn oil in a wok or frying pan and stir fry beef until well browned. Remove from pan and set aside. Add onion and green pepper and stir fry until golden. Remove and set aside with beef.

3 Drain black beans, crush to a paste with the garlic. If necessary, heat a little more oil in the pan, add paste and stir fry for 1 minute. Return beef and onion mixture to pan and stir well to combine.

4 To make sauce combine sugar, cornflour, soy sauce sherry and water, pour into pan and cook for 1-2 minutes longer. Season to taste with salt and black pepper. Serve immediately with fluffy white rice.

Serves 4

Ham Crêpes

250g (8oz) ham slices

315ml (10fl oz) double cream

freshly ground black pepper

grated nutmeg

125g (4oz) grated Gruyère or Emmenthaler cheese

30g (1oz) butter

Crêpes

155g (5oz) plain flour

pinch salt

3 eggs, beaten

125ml (4fl oz) milk mixed with 170ml (5¹/₂fl oz) water

1 tblspn brandy

15g (¹/₂oz) butter, melted

extra butter, for frying

1 To make crêpes, sift flour and salt into a mixing bowl. Make a well in the centre and beat in the eggs and milk mixture. Mix until smooth, then stir in the brandy and melted butter. Cover and set aside to stand for 1 hour.

2 Melt a little butter in a heavy frying pan over a medium heat and, using a soup ladle, pour in enough batter to thinly coat surface of pan, rotating the pan quickly so that the batter evenly covers the surface. Cook for 30 seconds or until tiny holes appear over the surface of the crêpe and it is pale golden underneath.

3 Use a spatula to free the crêpe edges, flip crêpe over and cook for 15 seconds longer. Turn the crêpe on to a plate and set aside. Continue with remaining batter to make 16 crêpes.

4 Preheat oven to 180°C (350°F/ Gas 4). Cut the ham into strips. Divide ham between crêpes and roll up. Arrange crêpes side-by-side in a buttered baking dish, pour over the cream and season to taste with black pepper and grated nutmeg. Sprinkle with cheese, dot with butter and bake for 15 minutes or until golden.

Makes 16 crêpes

Tikka Kebab

While this dish does require overnight marinating it has been included here because the initial preparation and the final cooking are both very quick.

750g (1¹/₂lb) boned lamb shoulder or leg, cut into 2.5cm (1in) cubes

juice of 1 lemon

140g (4¹/₂oz) natural yogurt

2 onions, chopped

3 cloves garlic, chopped

1 tblspn vinegar

¹/₂ tspn ground turmeric

¹/₂ tspn salt

1 tspn freshly ground black pepper

1 green or red pepper, cored, seeded and cut into 2.5cm (1in) squares

2 onions, quartered

1 lemon, quartered, for garnish

1 Place the lamb in a bowl and sprinkle with the lemon juice. Place the yogurt, chopped onions, garlic, vinegar, turmeric, salt and black pepper in a food processor or blender and process until mixture is blended. Pour over the lamb, toss to coat, cover and marinate overnight.

2 Thread the cubes of meat onto kebab skewers, alternating with the green or red pepper and quartered onions. Barbecue or grill the kebabs, turning frequently until golden brown and cooked through.

3 Serve hot, garnished with lemon quarters and accompanied by naan, the Indian flat bread or pitta bread. Brush bread with butter, then crisp under a grill. Serve with crisp green salad.

Serves 4-6

Grilled Trout

4 trout, cleaned

salt

freshly ground black pepper

15g (¹/₂oz) butter

4 spring onions, chopped

1 tblspn chopped fresh parsley

juice of ¹/₂ lemon

1 Season trout with salt and black pepper. Place butter, spring onions, parsley and lemon juice in a bowl and mix to combine. Spoon mixture into cavity of each trout.

2 Cook trout under a preheated medium grill for 5 minutes each side or until flesh flakes when tested with a fork. Arrange on a warm serving dish and serve immediately, garnished with lemon wedges.

Serves 4

Pan-fried Chicken with Lemon and Rosemary

6 boneless chicken breast fillets

2 tblspn plain flour

salt

freshly ground black pepper

60ml (2fl oz) olive oil

1 sprig fresh rosemary

1¹/₂ tspn grated lemon rind

2 tblspn juice lemon

extra fresh rosemary, for garnish

1 Wipe the chicken fillets with absorbent kitchen paper. Season flour with salt and black pepper to taste. Place flour and chicken fillets in a plastic food bag and shake to coat chicken with flour. Remove chicken from bag and shake off excess flour.

2 Heat oil with rosemary in a large frying pan over a low heat for 3 minutes. Increase heat, add chicken and cook for 3 minutes each side or until brown.

3 Add grated lemon rind and juice to pan, cover and cook over a low heat, turning several times, for 10 minutes or until chicken is cooked. Garnish with extra lemon rind and fresh rosemary and serve immediately.

Serves 6

Tikka Kebab

Index

Managing Editor: Rachel Blackmore
Editors: Kirsten John, Linda Venturoni
Production Manager: Sheridan Carter
Senior Production Editor: Anna Maguire
Production Editor: Sheridan Packer
Editorial and Production Assistant: Danielle Thiris
Layout and Finished Art: Stephen Joseph

Published by J.B. Fairfax Press Pty Limited
80-82 McLachlan Avenue
Rushcutters Bay, NSW 2011
A.C.N. 003 738 430

Formatted by J.B. Fairfax Press Pty Limited
Printed by Toppan Printing Co, Hong Kong
PRINTED IN HONG KONG

JBFP 376 A/UK
Includes Index
ISBN 1 86343 116 0 (set)
ISBN 1 86343 209 4

Distribution and Sales Enquiries
Australia: J.B. Fairfax Press Pty Limited
Ph: (02) 361 6366 Fax: (02) 360 6262
United Kingdom: J.B. Fairfax Press Limited
Ph: (0933) 402330 Fax: (0933) 402234